Jesus Restores All

*Good News from the Bible about
Heaven and Hell*

John Hopler

Unless otherwise noted, Scripture quotations are taken from the New American Standard Bible (1995 version).

ISBN for paperback: 978-1-965501-06-1

ISBN for hardcover: 978-1-965501-07-8

Table of Contents

Dedication

I dedicate this booklet to my Lord and Savior, Jesus Christ, who restored me to worship God; to my dear wife and best friend, Sandy, who has loved me like no other; and to my parents, Jack and Perle Hopler, who inspired me to believe in Jesus.

Introduction

This booklet tells the beautiful Jesus-Judgment-Victory gospel that *Jesus is the Savior of the whole world who, through His judgments, will victoriously restore everyone who ever lived to worship God.* Here is the story behind this booklet

I began to follow Jesus in 1973. I later became a full-time pastor. I served in four churches and with three interdenominational ministries that proclaimed the gospel of Jesus Christ throughout the world.

In 2014, I took two plane trips in which I talked with two people about Jesus. Each person asked me, *"What really happens to a person who dies without believing in Jesus?"* This led me to do a five-year study of the Bible and church history on this question.

All Christians agree that Jesus will judge unbelievers. But Christians disagree on what happens in that judgment. Will those who die as unbelievers suffer forever? Will they cease to exist? Will they be restored to God? You will get a different answer depending on the Christian who answers that question.

For 40 years I have been in a church culture that believed that Jesus in His judgments will subject those who die as unbelievers to never-ending suffering. If this is true, it means that 30-60-90% of humanity will suffer forever, separated from God and from their loved ones forever and ever.

After doing my study, I now believe that Jesus through His judgments will restore all to worship God (Rom. 14:9-11).

The belief that Jesus will restore all is the best news I have heard since I first believed in Jesus. Believing this beautiful gospel message has been so life-changing for me that I wrote this booklet.

I hope and pray that these 31 readings will lead you to a better knowledge of our loving God and a better understanding of the beautiful gospel of Jesus Christ.

God bless you!

John Hopler

1

The Question

"It is appointed for men to die once and after this comes judgment." Heb. 9:27

Think of an individual you know well who died without believing in Jesus Christ. That person might be a family member or a close friend or some other acquaintance. What *really* happened to that person who died as an unbeliever?

Christians agree that those who believe in Jesus are saved and have eternal life (John 3:16). Jesus will resurrect believers to life and unbelievers to judgment (John 5:29). So, there is a clear difference between believers who have eternal life and unbelievers who are judged.

But what is the final fate of those who are judged? For 1500 years most churches have taught that those who die without believing in Jesus will be judged and will suffer without end. This means that 30-60-90% of humanity will be in torment and separated from God and their loved ones forever and ever.

However, this view has never been universally accepted by Christians. In the early church, all believed in a future judgment. But many viewed that God's judgment is a loving correction to bring every single person into His kingdom. Here is their view of the future:

Jesus is the Savior who came to take away the sin of the world and to abolish death. (John 1:29; 2 Tim.1:10). Through His judgments Jesus will bring all under God's authority (1 Cor. 15:28). In the end, Jesus will restore all (Acts 3:21), reconcile all (Col. 1:20), and renew all with no more tears, suffering or sorrow of any kind (Rev. 21:4–5). In the end, every person who has ever lived will be immersed in the love of Jesus Christ with God being all in all (1 Cor. 15:28). Jesus will resurrect, judge, and restore our loved ones and all humanity to joyfully worship God in the end (Rom. 14: 9-11).

This picture would be wonderful. But is it true or is it a fantasy? *I personally think it is true.* But I did not always think so. The reason is I made a mistake.

2

My Mistake: Ignoring the Issue

"Now these people [the Bereans] were more noble-minded than those in Thessalonica, for they received the word with great eagerness, examining the Scriptures daily to see whether these things were so." Acts 17:11

Unlike the Bereans who carefully studied Paul's gospel (Acts 17:11), I had made a mistake. Though I have regularly read the Bible the last 50 years, it was not until 2014 that I seriously studied what happens to those who die as unbelievers. I thought of this illustration:

Imagine my friend is in a war overseas. One day, while getting ready to go to a church service, I see three soldiers on my porch. They all tell me my friend's plane was shot down. But one says he was captured by the opposing army and is likely in torment. The second soldier disputes this. He says my friend died in the plane crash. The third soldier disagrees. He says my friend escaped, is safe and is on a plane headed back home.

I would not say to the soldiers, *"This is interesting, but I have a church service to go to."* Knowing my friend's fate would be a priority for me. How much more am I to devote time and energy to finding out what happened to my loved ones who died as unbelievers?

Answering this question is very important. It affects our view of God. One view says God created mankind, knowing that 30-60-90% of humanity will be in never-ending torment. Another view is God will annihilate much of humanity. Another view of God is He will justly punish those who have done wrong but, in the end, like a loving Father, He will restore all. These are three different pictures of God!

So, I decided not to ignore this issue any longer. I decided to be like the Bereans and study this issue thoroughly. In my study, I realized I had made a second mistake—a premature diagnosis.

3

A Premature Diagnosis

"For it is written: 'As I live, says the Lord, to Me every knee will bow, and every tongue will give praise to God.'" Romans 14:11

I made a second mistake, like one a doctor made as to our son.

In 1993, Sandy and I took our infant son to the hospital to be evaluated. After some tests, the doctor said to us, "Your son has leukemia. We need to begin chemotherapy immediately."

Ninety minutes later, the doctor came and told us our son did not need chemotherapy. Although it *looked* like our son had leukemia, he did *not* have leukemia. The doctor, though good-hearted, made a mistake. She should have consulted with a pathologist before telling us our son had leukemia. But she did eventually consult with the pathologist who quickly overturned her mistaken diagnosis.

Like this doctor, I made a mistake. I assumed (like many but not all Christians) that Jesus will subject those who die as unbelievers to never-ending suffering. But this was a mistake—a premature diagnosis. I did not consider the possibility that God's judgments are restorative, with all worshiping God in the end, as many Scriptures indicate.

When the doctor told us our son had leukemia, we feared that we would lose our son. But when the doctor told us she had made a mistake, we leaped for joy. Similarly, based on my premature diagnosis, I had assumed that 30-60-90% of humanity who died as unbelievers would suffer forever. But when my wife and I discovered that all will worship God in the end, we leaped for joy again!

Do you have a loved one who died as an unbeliever? Then keep reading. You will leap for joy when you look at the Scriptures. That joy is not based on sentimental optimism but on facts.

4

A Look at the Facts

"Christ died for our sins according to the Scriptures, and He was buried, and He was raised on the third day according to the Scriptures." 1 Cor. 15:3-4

Years ago, my friend and I were sharing the message of Jesus Christ with a friend. Vince (not his real name) was a skeptic who loved to talk. He talked and talked and talked, insisting that Jesus did not rise from the dead. Then Vince stopped talking. During that moment of silence, my friend spoke up. He quietly declared: "No, Jesus did rise from the dead."

Pause. More silence.

My friend's calm and bold declaration that Jesus rose from the dead, coupled with his pause and silence, was like an explosion in the room. The three of us in the room were focused on this one simple fact: Jesus rose from the dead. Later that year, Vince put his faith in Jesus Christ.

Jesus *did* die on the Cross. It happened. Jesus *did* rise from the dead. It happened. If you and I had been in Jerusalem on the Friday that Christ was crucified and then placed in the tomb, we would have seen His body lying there. The next Sunday, if we had entered the tomb, we would have seen it empty.

Facts are facts are facts. Jesus' death and resurrection *are* facts.

If you come away from this book thinking, "*The author believes that in the end, Jesus through His judgments will restore all to worship God*" you have missed my point. It is not about what I think. It is about facts. My point is there is a reality. Our loved ones who die as unbelievers will either suffer forever, will cease to exist or will be restored to God. That reality will be seen when we see Jesus. So, our goal is to find facts.

As to what will really happen to people who die as unbelievers, there are some indisputable facts *all* Christians can *quickly* agree upon.

5

Three Indisputable Facts

"And if anyone's name was not found written in the book of life, he was thrown into the lake of fire." Rev. 20:15

Here are three *indisputable facts* Christians affirm:

First, Jesus, the Savior of the world, died for mankind's sins and rose again (1st Cor. 15:3-4). All Christians agree that Jesus paid for the sins of the world and rose again from the dead.

Second, Jesus will judge all people. Christians agree that only believers in Jesus Christ are saved (John 3:16; Acts 4:12). He will resurrect believers to life and unbelievers to be condemned (John 5:23, 29). Jesus will cast unbelievers into the lake of fire (Rev. 20:15; 21:8).

Third, Christians disagree on what happens to those in the lake of fire. Some believe they will suffer forever. Some believe they will cease to exist. Some believe they will be restored to God.

Consider this quote by the highly respected theologian Millard Erikson:

"The discussion of the topics considered in this book [final fate of unbelievers] *is also important because they have never received definitive treatment by the church. No official council has given them the concerted attention and authoritative ruling that were given to such doctrines as the person of Christ and the Trinity...The question of how many will be saved and the ultimate destiny of the lost, or the duration of punishment for unbelievers did not receive such attention."* [1]

I interacted with Dr. Erickson, and he confirmed his quote. He acknowledged that Christians disagree on what happens to those who die as unbelievers.

God will judge unbelievers. That is a fact. But it is also a fact that not every Christian believes that those who die as unbelievers will suffer forever.

---

[1] Erickson, *How Shall They Be Saved?* (Grand Rapids, Michigan: Baker Books, 1996) p. 26.

6

Never-Ending Justice Principle

"The one who believes in the Son has eternal life, but the one who does not obey the Son will not see life, but the wrath of God remains on him." John 3:36

I need to clear up a (possible) point of confusion. There is a difference between the Never-Ending Justice Principle and the Never-Ending Suffering Scenario.

Here's the Never-Ending Justice Principle: *"If a person is unrepentant and unbelieving in Christ, then that person will be separated from God as long as he or she is unrepentant."* God will not allow the unrepentant into His kingdom (John 3:36; 1 Cor. 6:9-11).

In contrast, here's the Never-Ending Suffering Scenario: *"If a person dies without trusting in Christ (through hearing the gospel, or through a dream or general revelation), then that person will consciously suffer forever with no hope of any remedy or relief."* This is different than the truth that the unrepentant are presently separated from God.

There are three views of what happens to those in the lake of fire. Some think they are tormented forever. Some think they are annihilated forever. Some think they are restored to praise God forever.

Do all three views agree that Jesus is the only way to salvation? Yes.

Do all three views agree that only those who are repentant are saved? Yes.

Do all three views agree that Jesus will judge mankind? Yes.

Do all three views agree that unbelievers will be cast into the lake of fire? Yes!

All three agree on these four key points. But they disagree on the ultimate and never-ending fate of those in the lake of fire.

This begs the question: Why do some people believe that those in the lake of fire will be in never-ending torment?

7

Never-Ending Torment View

"These will go away into eternal punishment, but the righteous into eternal life." Matthew 25:46

This verse is the main one used to support the claim that some will suffer forever and ever. However, the Greek word for *eternal* (*aiōnios*) does not mean *never-ending* but *age-enduring* or *of the world to come.*[2] So *eternal punishment* means *punishment in the world to come* or *divine punishment for an indefinite period that is open-ended.*

In Luke 16:19-31 Jesus tells of a rich man in torment in Hades. But He does not say the rich man was in torment forever. Also, Hades is the intermediate state before eternal judgment and is later thrown into the lake of fire (Rev. 20:14). After Hades is destroyed, what was the rich man's fate? Luke 16 gives no answer.

---

[2] Vincent's Word Studies, https://www.studylight.org/commentaries/eng/vnt/2-thessalonians-1.html.

A third passage is Revelation 20:11-15 where the unrighteous are thrown into the lake of fire (v. 15). But there is no "Revelation 20:16" that teaches that those in the lake of fire are in torment forever.

Will there be a serious judgment of unbelievers? Yes. But Matthew 25:46, Luke 16, and Revelation 20 do not present an indisputable case for the never-ending suffering view.

If someone had the burden to prove from the Bible that a person who dies as an unbeliever will suffer forever, that person would not meet that burden of proof.

To subject people to never-ending suffering is out of character for the God of kindness and love. If the never-ending torment view is true, you would expect God to warn mankind constantly from Genesis to Revelation. But this warning is absent from the Scriptures. The fact that God does not explicitly state that unbelievers will suffer forever caused me to dig a little deeper. When I did, God opened my eyes.

8

Eye-Opener # 1

Doctrine of Reserve

"It is the glory of God to conceal a matter."
Proverbs 25:2

No quote opened my eyes more than one by Alexander Mack (1679–1735). Mack was the founder of the German Baptist Brethren. There are hundreds of churches today that are the fruit of Mack's ministry.

Here is an interchange between Mack and his son about unbelievers:

Father: They will have to listen as Christ says: "Depart from me, you cursed, into the eternal fire prepared for the devil and his angels..." // If anyone's name is not found in the book of life, he will be thrown into the lake of fire, where the worm does not die and the fire will not be quenched (Rev. 20:15; Mark 9:48; Isa. 66:24).

Son: Do tell me, are these torments and tortures to last for eternity, without end?

Father: That it should last for eternity is not supported by Holy Scripture. It is not necessary to talk much about it or speculate about it...Therefore, that is a much better and more blessed gospel which teaches how to escape the wrath of God than the gospel which teaches that eternal punishment has an end. Even though this is true, it should not be preached as a gospel to the godless.[3]

Does eternal punishment have an end? What did Mack mean?

Mack believed Jesus will restore all in the end. But Mack practiced the *doctrine of reserve.* He believed God wanted to conceal this truth from unbelievers and reserved it for mature Christians. Mack did not preach universalism. Instead, he *shouted* Jesus' gospel and His fierce judgment and *whispered* to mature Christians that Jesus will restore all.

---

[3] Donald F. Durnbaugh, *European Origins of the Brethren: A Source Book on the Beginnings of the Church of the Brethren in the Early Eighteenth Century* (Elgin, IL: Brethren Press, 1958), 398–99.

9

Eye-Opener # 2

Church Orthodoxy

*"He will come again in glory to judge the living
and the dead and his kingdom will have no end."
Nicene Creed (381 AD)*

My second eye-opener was learning that the
belief that Jesus will restore all *is* (arguably) the
most orthodox view.

All agree that the Nicene Creed is orthodox. That
creed is generally accepted by the universal
church today, including Catholics, Orthodox,
Anglican and Protestants.[4] Notice that the
Nicene Creed does not teach that those who die
as unbelievers will suffer forever. It just teaches
that Jesus will judge the living and the dead.

Gregory of Nyssa (335-394) was a "father to the
fathers," the leading contributor to the revised
Nicene Creed. He believed Jesus would restore
all to worship God:

---

[4] Britannica, T. Editors of Encyclopedia, "Nicene
Creed," *Encyclopedia Britannica*

"For it is evident that God will in truth be 'in all' when there shall be no evil in existence, when every created being is at harmony with itself, and every tongue shall confess that Jesus Christ is Lord."[5]

That Gregory, the leading contributor to this Creed, believed God would restore all suggests his belief was orthodox.

Also, there is an X Factor: The *doctrine of reserve*. Many who believed that God would save all did not want this taught publicly for pastoral reasons. So, if the restoration of all was the orthodox view, it makes sense that it would not have been included in the Nicene Creed. But if the never-ending suffering view was the orthodox view, it surely would have been included in the Nicene Creed. These factors suggest that Gregory's belief in the restoration of all, not the never-ending suffering view, is the *most* orthodox.

---

[5] Tentmaker Ministries, "The Church Fathers" https://www.tentmaker.org/Quotes/churchfathersquotes.htm.

10

Eye-Opener # 3

The Moravians

"Peter Böhler, one of the Moravian brethren, in order to make out universal redemption, lately frankly confessed in a letter that all the damned souls would hereafter be brought out of hell." [6]

A third eye-opening quote is this one about the Moravian American Bishop, Peter Böhler (1712–1775). This quote is from George Whitefield's letter to John Wesley. Bohler introduced the Wesleys to justification by faith. This was a catalyst to the Methodist movement.

The early Moravians are famous for their around-the-clock prayer meeting that lasted one hundred years.[7] The Moravians are also known for their zeal in missions. C. H. Robinson noted that by 1915, the Moravians had sent out three thousand missionaries, one for every twelve

---

[6] Tentmaker, "Peter Böhler."
[7] Leslie K. Tarr, "A Prayer Meeting that Lasted 100 Years," *Christianity Today*.

members, compared to one missionary for every two thousand members in English churches.[8]

Bohler and the Moravians' zeal was tied into their view of God. They had a triumphant message that fueled a triumphant faith that led to a triumphant mission. This message portrays Christ as triumphant in every imaginable way and inspires us in our missionary endeavors. They believed that Jesus Christ forgives all, restores all, and reconciles all.

If the Leader of this mission (Jesus Christ) is victorious in restoring all in the end, then, like the Moravians, our mission will be victorious as well.

The fact that zealous missionaries like Bohler and Mack believed that Jesus would restore all was eye-opening to me. This refuted the argument that only immature Christians believed in the restoration of all.

---

[8] C. H. Robinson, *History of Christian Missions* (Edinburgh: T&T Clark, 1915), 50.

11

Eye-Opener # 4

Pastors' Private Beliefs

"What you hear whispered in your ear, proclaim on the housetops." Matt. 10:27

A fourth eye-opener came in my private talks with pastors. Almost all pastors I have talked with have doubts about the never-ending suffering view. But they are not public about their doubts.

I asked myself, "If the never-ending suffering view is true, why aren't pastors teaching this regularly? And if they have doubts about this view, why are they being quiet about those doubts?"

I have observed three factors that affect pastors:

First, many are like me who have not taken the time to seriously study this issue. They mistakenly assumed the Bible clearly taught the never-ending suffering view. Or they mistakenly assumed the never-ending suffering view was the unanimous teaching of the early church. Or they were too busy with church work to take time to study what is (in their mind) a controversial issue.

Second, pastors have an anti-retraction bias. To re-evaluate a statement of faith on a public website threatens their credibility with church members. No one is motivated to study a topic where they have to admit that they made a mistake. So, they tend to avoid this issue.

Third, many pastors who privately question the never-ending suffering view are (sadly) pressured into silence. Because they fear losing their jobs or the respect of others, they keep quiet.

But this is changing today (in large part) because of the Internet. There is a grassroots movement of Christians who are learning about (and embracing and teaching) the belief that Jesus will restore all. This is like the first century when Jesus chose common people like Peter and Mary Magdalene to proclaim a new message about God.

12

Eye-Opener # 5

Mistreatment by Institutions

"A single friar who goes counter to all Christianity for a thousand years must be wrong." Emperor Charles V [9]

When Martin Luther claimed the Pope's teaching violated God's word, he was opposed by the Pope and the Emperor. In church history, those following Jesus closely have often been mistreated by religious leaders.

Some adherents to the never-ending torment view label those who hope in the restoration of all as "heretics" or "unbiblical." They claim, like Emperor Charles, that those who go counter to church tradition must be wrong. This led me to ask, "Will those who believe in ultimate restoration be praised for their commitment to the Scriptures, like Luther, in future generations?"

_____

[9] https://lineagejourney.com/timeline-details/event/the-diet-of-worms

Many who hope in ultimate restoration today are shunned by organized church leaders. I have talked to many dear believers who are told they cannot be part of a church or church association because they embrace the same hope as many of the early Christians.

Many who proclaim the Nicene Creed would not permit its main writer, Gregory of Nyssa, to be a member of their church! Many who are the spiritual great-grandchildren of Mack and Bohler would shun them as heretics!

William Paley, the Christian apologist, warned against: *"Contempt before investigation."*[10] I thought, "Maybe I have misunderstood the Scriptures. Maybe Jesus' judgment of humanity will lead to the victorious result of all humanity worshipping God in the end."

So, I decided to take a fresh look at the Scriptures.

---

[10] William Paley, *A View of the Evidences of Christianity* (London: Faulder, 1794).

13

The Glorious Gospel of Jesus

"The glorious gospel." 1 Timothy 1:11

I used to frame the gospel as a *heaven-or-hell test*: *"You either go to heaven or to hell forever. To avoid hell, believe in Jesus."* But after taking a fresh look at the Scriptures I saw a different framing of the gospel.

The Biblical gospel is a "Jesus-centered" story of restoration. The gospel is about Christ the Victor restoring all that was lost by Adam:

God created Adam and Eve (Gen. 1:26) who sinned and brought death into the world (Rom. 5:12). But God planned to restore humanity to a life of worshipful obedience (Acts 3:21; Rom. 5:17). God promised that all the families of the earth would be blessed (Gen. 12:3) and that all people would worship and obey God (Ps. 22:27–29; Isa. 45:22–23).

God then sent His Son, Jesus Christ to take away the sin of the world (John 1:29). Jesus Christ died and rose from the dead (1 Cor. 15:3-4). Those who believe in Jesus receive eternal life (John 3:16). Believers are called to be His obedient disciples as part of God's plan to bring all people into the obedience of Christ, by the power of the Holy Spirit (Matt. 28:18–20; Acts 1:8).

Jesus will resurrect the righteous and the unrighteous (Acts 24:15), and He will judge all people (Rom. 2:6–9). Those who believe in Christ will not be condemned but will have eternal life (John 5:24, 29). The unrighteous will be resurrected to judgment (John 5:29) and cast into the lake of fire (Rev. 20:15).

Because Jesus did not come to judge the world but to save the world His judgments are part of His ultimate plan to save people (John 12:47). Through His judgments, Jesus will be victorious in restoring what Adam lost, with every knee bowing and every tongue giving joyful and voluntary praise to God (Rom. 14:9-11). In the end, God will be all in all (1 Cor. 15:28).

But some say, "God's judgments are very fierce. Aren't they intended to condemn sin?" Yes. But God's judgments must be read in the context of His plan to save the world.

14

Judgment and Restoration

"I did not come to judge the world but to save the world." John 12:47

As John 12:47 teaches, Jesus' heart is to save, not to destroy or to torment. His ultimate purpose in His judgments is to fulfill His mission to save the world.

I thought, "Some verses do not seem restorative but seem to condemn." But then I realized, it is not *either/or* but *both/and*. God's judgments strongly warn, severely condemn and victoriously restore. Some verses emphasize God's warnings and condemnation of sin. Other verses reveal God's restoration of sinners. Here's an example.

In Jeremiah 48, for 46 verses God rails against the evils of Moab. He says, *"I will make an end of Moab"* (48:35) and *"Moab will be destroyed from being a people"* (48:42). Yet Jeremiah 48 ends with God's promise to *"restore the fortunes of*

Moab in the latter days" (48:47). How can God *"make an end to Moab"* and *"destroy Moab from being a people,"* and still restore Moab's fortunes in the latter days? Answer: The Moabites who no longer exist will be restored in the next life. So, Moab's *end* (God's fierce judgment, vv. 1-46) was not the *ultimate end.* The ultimate end is God's larger heavenly story when God restores all.

Paul brought a church discipline on an immoral man (1 Cor. 5). Paul did not mince words: *"Remove the wicked man from among yourselves"* (v.11). But Paul also wrote: *"I have decided to turn such a person over to Satan for the destruction of his body, so that his spirit may be saved on the day of the Lord"* (5:5). Later the man did repent (2 Cor. 2:4–10). So, though Paul used fierce judgment language *("Remove the wicked man"),* God's judgments were used to restore the immoral man.

The ultimate plan of Jesus Christ, the Savior of the world, is to recover all. As I climbed "All Mountain" I saw God's plan more clearly.

15

All Mountain—Part I

"In you all the families of the earth shall be blessed." Genesis 12:3

I came to *All Mountain*—the mountain of verses from Genesis to Revelation that point to God blessing *all* and *all* worshipping God.

God promised to bless all the families of the earth (Gen. 12:3). If a family of six has four in heaven and two are in never-ending torment, is that family *truly* blessed? I don't think so. He promises to bless the *whole* family.

Psalm 22:27: "*All* the ends of the earth shall remember and turn to the Lord, and *all* the families of the nations shall worship before You."

Psalm 86:9: "*All* the nations You have made shall come and worship before You, O Lord."

Psalm 138:4-5: "*All* the kings of the earth will give thanks to You, O Lord, when they have heard the words of Your mouth."

Psalm 145:9, 21: "The Lord is good to *all*, and His mercy is over *all* that He has made... *All* flesh will bless His holy name forever and ever."

Isaiah 25: 8: "He will swallow up death forever; and the Lord God will wipe away tears from *all* faces."

Romans 5:18: "So then as through one transgression there resulted condemnation to *all* men, even so through one act of righteousness there resulted justification of life to *all* men."

Romans 14:11: "'As I live, says the Lord, *every* knee shall bow to Me, and *every* tongue shall give *praise to God*'."

1 Corinthians 15:22: "For as in Adam all die, so also in Christ shall *all* be made alive."

1 Corinthians 15:28: "When *all* things are subjected to Him, then the Son Himself will also be subjected to Him who puts *all* things in subjection under Him, that God may be *all* in *all*."

In the next reading I share more verses from All Mountain.

16

All Mountain—Part II

"Through Him to reconcile to Himself all things, whether on earth or in heaven, making peace by the blood of his cross." Col. 1:19-20

God plans to reconcile *all* things to Himself. Here are two more verses:

1 Timothy 4:10: "We have fixed our hope on the living God, who is the Savior of *all* men, especially those who believe." (*God saves all in the end, but He saves in a special way those who believe now.*)

Revelation 5:13: "And I heard *every* creature in heaven and on earth and under the earth and in the sea, and *all* that is in them, saying, 'To Him who sits on the throne and to the Lamb be blessing and honor and glory and might forever and ever!'"

Some say the word *all* doesn't mean each person but all types of people (e.g. Gentiles and Jews). While the word *all* can be used this way, the verses of all worshiping God do not give that picture. For example, see Isaiah 54:13: *"All your sons will be taught by the Lord; and the well-being of your sons will be great."* Was Isaiah suggesting just *some* of Israel's sons would have well-being?

Jesus loves each person. Doesn't it make sense that Jesus will succeed in saving all that was lost through Adam? Is the issue the definition of the word *all?* Or is the issue our faith that Jesus will be successful in doing what was promised in the *All Mountain* verses?

Others say the verses that describe every knee bowing and every tongue confessing Jesus as Lord do not mean people will worship Him voluntarily but from compulsion. But each of the 10 times in the Bible the Greek word for *give praise* (*exomologeō*) in Romans 14:11 is used, it refers to someone making a voluntary, not forced, confession.

As I embraced a childlike faith in my loving God and Father, I began expecting that Jesus will bring all to worship Christ in eternity.

17

God's Character—Part I

"Father, forgive them, for they do not know what they are doing." Luke 23:34

Consider this illustration.

"Suppose you work at a store and you catch a teen shoplifting. You happen to know the father very well. He is loving and just and is committed to raising his son to obey Jesus. The next day, you talk with three employees, Alan, Bob, and Carl. Alan thinks the father beat his son for shoplifting. Bob speculates the father kicked his son out of the house. Carl believes the father restored him. The three ask for your opinion. You would likely say "I do not have the facts. The father did not tell me what he did. But based on what I know of the father's character, I think the father did what would restore his son."

As in this illustration, there is no explicit word from God that describes from start to finish what happens to unbelievers after they die. But we do know God.

God is all-knowing and all-powerful. He created human beings, knowing that they would disobey Him. Do you think He casts them into the lake of fire to torment them forever? Or do you think the lake of fire is part of His sovereign and loving plan to restore all things?

God's character is best seen in His Son Jesus Christ. Christ's death shows that God is both just and loving and that His love has no limits. When Jesus died on the cross, He asked God to forgive His enemies (Luke 23:34). His resurrection shows His power has no limits.

When looking at Jesus, His death and His resurrection, I connected the dots. I connected God's loving and powerful character with God's judgment of unbelievers with the future events described in the All Mountain verses of all worshiping God.

More than anything, my view of God's character as seen in the person of Jesus Christ is the foundation for me believing that Jesus will restore all.

18

God's Character—Part II

"His anger is for a moment and His favor is for a lifetime." Ps. 30:4

When I looked closely at God's character, I believed He will restore all. Some say, *"God's favor is for a moment and His anger is for eternity."* But that contradicts Psalm 30:4. It is His love that last forever, not His anger.

Here are some other verses:

"The Lord's acts of mercy do not end" (Lam. 3:22). This indicates God's mercy extends forever...even after we die.

"Behold the Lamb of God who takes away the sin of the world" (John 1:29). Did Jesus take away all sin or not?

"Where sin abounds, grace abounds even more" (Rom. 5:20). We cannot out-sin the grace of God. God's grace will win out in eternity.

"Mercy triumphs over judgment." (James 2:13). God judges—but His judgments are part of His plan to show mercy to all. And mercy triumphs over judgment.

God desires all to be saved (1 Tim 2:4) and has all power (Matt. 19:26). This led me to believe that God will save all.

"Love your enemies" (Matt. 5:44). Yes, people are evil. But God commands us to love even our enemies as Jesus demonstrated in His death on the cross. God practices what He preaches. He loves all people.

"He who did not spare His own Son but delivered Him up for us all, how will He not also with Him freely give us all things?" (Rom. 8:32). God promises to freely give us all things. "All things" includes people: *"All things belong to you, whether Paul or Apollos or Cephas or the world."* (1 Cor. 3:21-23). Is it not reasonable to think God will give us our loved ones who died as unbelievers?

Jesus came to give us good news. That good news is explained in detail in the book of Romans.

19

The Book of Romans

"So all Israel will be saved." Rom. 11: 26

Paul was a missionary to the Gentiles. A question they had was: *What happened to our loved ones who died without believing in Jesus?* Paul answered this question in his letter to the Romans.

He first explains we are justified by faith and sanctified by the Spirit (Chapters 1-8). Then in chapters 9-11, Paul addresses the question, *What about the Jews?* In so doing Paul also addresses the question, *What about our unbelieving relatives?* Paul writes about **his** unbelieving relatives—**his** kinsfolk, the Jews (9:3).

After reproving Israel for not believing in Jesus, Paul writes: *"For I do not want you, brethren, to be uninformed of this mystery—so that you will not be wise in your own estimation—that a partial hardening has happened to Israel until the fullness of the Gentiles has come in, and so all* Israel will be saved" (Rom. 11:25–26, emphasis mine).

Notice that it is only a *partial* hardening. For, in the end, *all* Israel will be saved. How? Romans 11:26–27 gives the answer: *"The Deliverer will come from Zion; He will remove ungodliness from Jacob. This is My covenant with them, when I take away their sins."* All Israel will be saved when God *"removes ungodliness from Jacob."* This is not a lenient God who lets people into heaven, but a powerful God who takes away the sin of Jacob through His judgments.

Paul then writes, *"The gifts and the calling of God are irrevocable"* (11:29). God made irrevocable promises to the Jews (and to all the families in the earth in Genesis 12:3) that He will fulfill in the next life. So, Paul writes that God will *"show mercy to all"* (11:32).

The first-century Jews saw their own kin Jesus in person and rejected Him. Yet *"All Israel will be saved."* How much more will God save our unbelieving loved ones who never saw Jesus in person?

Paul never talked about hell. So, what is hell?

20

What About Hell?

"He will save His people from their sins."
Matthew 1:21

In my study, I realized that the picture of hell I had in my mind was different than the hell described by Jesus.

The English word "hell" is the Greek word *gehenna*. It is a transliteration of the Valley of Hinnom, which was the place of judgment when the Babylonians conquered Jerusalem, as Jeremiah prophesied (Jer. 7:30-31).

A common statement is Jesus talked about hell more than anyone. That's true. Jesus is the only one in the New Testament (except James in James 3:6) who utters the word *gehenna*. Jesus was referring to the judgment on Israel in 70 AD just as the judgment from the Babylonians centuries before. First century Jews would have understood Jesus' reference to the Babylonian judgment.

Is there also a judgment in the next life?

Yes. But when Jesus talked about hell (gehenna), He was primarily referring to the judgment in 70 AD on Israel for rejecting Him as the Messiah. But like many others, I had taken these verses about gehenna (hell) and imagined an inaccurate picture of the afterlife. This led to this distorted picture of Jesus:

Knock, knock. Who's there?

It's Jesus. Let me in. Why?

To save you. Save me from what?

From the never-ending suffering that I will inflict on you if you don't let me in.

There is no verse that says Jesus came to save us from a hell of never-ending suffering. Instead, as Matthew 1:21 states, Jesus came to save us from sin.

Will we suffer if we continue to sin? Yes. Will Jesus cast sinners into the lake of fire? Yes. But the lake of fire is part of Jesus' overall plan to save all from sin. How did the never-ending suffering view become the main view? For this, we need to look at church history.

21

Church History-Part I

"In the beginning the church was a fellowship of men and women centering on the living Christ. Then the church moved to Greece where it became a philosophy. Then it moved to Rome where it became an institution. Next, it moved to Europe, where it became a culture. And, finally, it moved to America where it became an enterprise." Former U.S. Senate Chaplain Richard Halverson[11]

This quote gives some insight into how the church developed over the years.

In the early church the view that God would restore all was either the orthodox and majority view or an accepted hope.

Then philosophical approaches held sway over a child-like approach to believe God, as our loving Father.

---

[11] "Richard Halverson Quotes and Sayings–Page 1, https://www.inspiringquotes.us/author/5825-richard-halverson.

A change occurred with Augustine. In his day, the belief that God would restore all was prevalent. He acknowledged that *"There are very many in our day, who though not denying the Holy Scriptures, do not believe in endless torments."*[12] But Augustine, who was not proficient in the Greek language, misinterpreted Matthew 25:46. He said that *eternal punishment* means *punishment that lasts forever* rather than *punishment in the age to come*.

Then the church was institutionalized and was aligned with the government. Government rulers (especially Justinian in the 6th century) chose Augustine's view as a deterrent to lawlessness.

When the spiritually powerful early church turned into a materially powerful institutional church, those in power said that Jesus will subject 30-60-90% of humanity to never-ending suffering.

---

[12] Augustine, *Enchiridion*, CXII.

22

Church History-Part II

"In the beginning the church was a fellowship of men and women centering on the living Christ....... Next, it moved to Europe, where it became a culture. And, finally, it moved to America where it became an enterprise." Former U.S. Senate Chaplain Richard Halverson[13]

In the early church, a prevailing belief was that Jesus would restore all. Later the institutional church adopted Augustine's misinterpretation of Matthew 25:46 and began teaching the never-ending suffering view.

The never-ending suffering view was taught to keep people in order. The picture of a never-ending hell was embedded into the culture and into people's minds through art forms such as literature, music, and paintings.

---

[13] "Richard Halverson Quotes and Sayings–Page 1,"https://www.inspiringquotes.us/author/5825-richard-halverson.

Then, when the church came to America, it became an enterprise. The never-ending suffering view has been used as a motivation to grow churches and to raise funds for missions. When pastors have doubts about this view, they are reluctant to share their doubts because they do not want to lose their jobs. It is contrary to a pastor's business inclinations to retract what is written in a statement of faith, for fear of people losing confidence in the leaders. So, the never-ending suffering view is not carefully examined by those in leadership and becomes the default position.

Simply put, institutional and economic biases have resulted in a false depiction of Jesus, that He will subject most or a major segment of created humanity to never-ending suffering.

But many today are humbly acknowledging these biases. Many are taking a fresh look at the Bible to see that Jesus restores all.

23

The Broad Road

"Enter through the narrow gate; for the gate is wide and the way is broad that leads to destruction, and there are many who enter through it. For the gate is narrow and the way is constricted that leads to life, and there are few who find it." Matt. 7:13-14

Some ask, "If Jesus will restore all, how do you explain this passage?"

Jesus is talking about two ways to live our lives: The narrow gate and the wide gate.

Jesus' exhortation to enter through the narrow gate was His way to build obedient disciples. Only a few enter the kingdom through the narrow gate by living a life of obedience and love. Those who obey Jesus experience life now and life in the world to come. They are resurrected to life (John 5:29).

But most enter through the wide gate that leads to destruction. They choose a path of unbelief and disobedience and experience destruction in this life. If they stay on that broad road in this life, they will be resurrected to judgment and cast into the lake of fire (Rev. 20:15).

But the purpose of God's judgment is to build obedient followers who worship God (Rom. 14:9-11).

Notice this: *Those who enter through the narrow gate and those who enter through the wide gate **both enter.*** At issue is *how* (through which gate) they enter the kingdom of God.

So, rather than *denying* that God will restore all, Matthew 7:13-14 *points* to God restoring all.

Jesus wants us to enter through the narrow gate, not the wide gate, the broad road. But whether a person enters God's kingdom through the narrow gate or through the wide gate, the good news is that Jesus, our loving and all-powerful Savior, will restore all in the end, with all worshiping God and with God being all in all (Rom. 14:9-11; 1 Cor. 15:28).

24

What About Free Will?

"The king's heart is like channels of water in the hands of the Lord. He turns it whichever way He wishes." Prov. 21:1

How can God restore all if each person has free will? Answer: God can accomplish His sovereign purposes while preserving each person's free will.

We are not robots. To be with God each person must voluntarily choose Him. *But God's teaching ability is greater than our teachability.* God works masterfully so that people voluntarily choose Him.

God's transforming love includes bringing painful discipline on those He loves. God, the wise Father, can effectively teach, train and discipline all people to follow Him (Pr. 22:15).

God's loving discipline can soften even the heart of proud kings (Pr. 21:1). God humbled Nebuchadnezzar, the evil Gentile king who led the Jews into captivity (Daniel 4). God also humbled Manasseh, the worst Jewish king (2 Kings 21:11; 2 Chron. 33:11-13). If the Lord was able to turn the hearts of these two proud kings to voluntarily worship God, He can turn anyone's heart.

In Revelation 20:15, those cast into the lake of fire certainly included the kings of the earth, Christ's enemies (Rev.19:19). In the next chapter, John writes: "The nations will walk by its light, *and the kings of the earth will bring their glory into it*." (Rev. 21:24). So, in Revelation 21, after the lake of fire judgment in Revelation 20, these proud kings are seen worshipping God!

Revelation 21:24 fulfills the promise in Psalm 138:4-5: *"All the kings of the earth will give thanks to Thee, O Lord when they have heard the words of Your mouth. And they will sing of the ways of the Lord."* Notice it does not say *some* of the kings, but *all* the kings are *"singing of the ways of the Lord."* God can really transform the heart of anyone to make a voluntary choice to worship God.

25

What about the Elect?

"God's electing grace calls into being a people charged with the responsibility of being the bearers of His universal salvation... To be chosen, to be elect, therefore does not mean that the elect are the saved and the rest are the lost. To be the elect in Christ Jesus, and there is no other election, means to be incorporated into His mission to the world, to be the bearer of God's saving purpose for His whole world, to be the sign and the agent and the first fruit of His blessed kingdom which is for all." Theologian Lesslie Newbigin [14]

I used to think the elect are the only ones to be saved forever. But the elect are the *first* to be saved. As the above quote explains, to be elect means to be chosen as God's representative to fulfill God's purpose at that time in history. Israel was God's elect in the Old Testament. The plan was *not* that Israel would be the *only* nation to

[14] Newbigin, *The Gospel in a Pluralist Society* (Grand Rapids, MI: Eerdmans, 1987), 86–87.

worship God, but the *first* to worship God (Isa. 19:24–25). Now believers in Jesus are God's elect representatives to the world. *Simply put, the elect exist **for** the non-elect.*

This explanation of election, combined with verses that describe all worshiping God, *points* to Jesus restoring all.

Consider the following illustration. A pastor concludes a Christmas Eve service by lighting the candles of the ushers. As such, the ushers are the elect (and others are not the elect) to have their candles lit. But the ushers are chosen, not as the *only* ones to have lit candles, but as the *first* to have lit candles. For a short moment, the ushers are the only ones in the room with lit candles. But this is only a temporary moment on a timeline which ends with **all** people in the room having lit candles.

So, God elects some to be the first to worship God forever. Their role is to be witnesses for Jesus Christ so that all will praise God.

26

Why Evangelize?

"Let everything that has breath praise the Lord."
Ps. 150: 6

I wondered, "Why urge people to believe in Jesus now if God will save all?" Psalm 150:6 gives the answer: *We evangelize so that all will praise God* ***now.***

The main reason to evangelize is Jesus Christ Himself. Having a relationship with Jesus is the best thing in the world. It is like my relationship with Sandy. I asked her to marry me in 1976 and she said "No." A year later I learned that Sandy had affections for me. Another person wanted me to know this so that I could have a relationship with Sandy immediately. So, I rushed to Sandy and again asked her to marry me—and she said, "Yes." I'm glad I did not wait!

Also, there is sadness for those who do not follow Jesus in this life. Paul wrote, *"If we deny Him, He will deny us" (2 Tim. 2:12).*

Those who reject Christ will suffer in this life, be resurrected to judgment, and cast into the lake of fire. We are warned to avoid sin now and to avoid the second death, the lake of fire (Rev. 2:11). This is a sound reason to believe in Jesus now.

Also, there are rewards in the next life depending on how we respond to Jesus in this life. We are told *"If we endure, we will also reign with Him"* (2 Tim. 2:12). There is no promise that unbelievers in this life will reign with Him. The prodigal son was restored to the family—but only the faithful older son was told *"All that is mine is yours"* (Luke 15:31).

But the main reason to evangelize is so all people will know God now and praise Him now. Psalm 150:6 is the last verse in the Psalms. Why wait until the next life for all to praise God?

So, why do we evangelize? In one word: Love. We evangelize, not because of a never-ending hell, but because we love God and we love people.

Love fills this world when all praise God *now*.

27

Missionary Sacrifice

"Join with me in suffering for the gospel."
2 Timothy 1:8

Some say: "Fewer missionaries will make sacrifices if there is no never-ending hell." Here are some responses.

First, many Christians (e.g. Origen) and missionaries (e.g. Moravians) believed Jesus would restore all, and they suffered for their faith. Second, missionaries can still be motivated to warn unbelievers about the lake of fire. Third, many non-Christians sacrificially do humanitarian work without any thought of a never-ending hell.

The message that God will subject 30-60-90% of humanity to never-ending suffering hurts missionary efforts. As an example, consider these words from Francis Xavier (1506-1552) who was a missionary to Japan:

"One of the things that most of all pains and torments these Japanese is, that we teach them that the prison of hell is irrevocably shut so that there is no egress therefrom. For they grieve over the fate of their departed children, of their parents, and relatives, and they often show their grief by their tears. So, they ask if there is any hope, any way to free them by prayer from that eternal misery, and I am obliged to answer that there is absolutely none."[15]

Francis Xavier, though well-meaning, preached a message that was half good news (the believers were saved) and half tragedy (their loved ones would suffer forever). In contrast, the Moravian missionary Peter Bohler shared a gospel that was 100% good news: Jesus will save us now and will restore all of humanity to worship God in the end.

The news that Jesus will restore all is good news worth sacrificing for!

---

[15] St. Francis Xavier, 1552 letter, cited in Sarris, *Heaven's Doors*, 190.

28

What about
Postmortem Salvation?

"We can set no limits to the agency of the Redeemer to redeem, to rescue, to discipline in His work, and so will He continue to operate after this life." Clement of Alexandria (150-215)[16]

For Jesus to restore all, He must save people after they die, as Clement believed. But my church culture has assumed otherwise: *"No doctrine* [that there is no post-mortem salvation] *even comes close to a) being so strongly believed by so many evangelicals despite b) being so utterly disastrous in its consequences and c) having so little by way of Scriptural support."*[17]

Jesus is Lord of both the dead and the living (Rom. 14:9). He holds the keys to Hades, the place of the dead (Rev. 1:18) because He plans to use those keys!

---

[16] Clement, *Stromata*, 5:14.90.4–91.2.
[17] Keith DeRose
"https://campuspress.yale.edu/keithderose/1129-2/.

If a person must be born again to be in God's kingdom (John 3:3) and if those who die as infants are in heaven, then regeneration must happen *after* these infants die. If so, why can't God regenerate adults after they die?

Why is there no example in the Bible of someone repenting and believing God after death? Because God is good and wise. If there is no postmortem salvation, a good God would have warned us, *"You must believe in Jesus before you die or you will suffer forever."* But this explicit warning is not in the Bible. However, if God plans to bring people into obedience after they die, it makes sense that God, in His wisdom, would be silent, lest people delay in obeying Jesus today.

So, why can we assume God will save people after death? Because we know from the Bible that God is loving, wise and all powerful and we know that all will praise God in the end (Romans 14:11).

29

How Clear is the Bible that Jesus will Restore All?

"I know whom I have believed." 2 Timothy 1:12

While the Bible could be clearer, the Bible is clear enough for me to reasonably hope and expect Jesus will restore all. The Bible is clear that God is loving and all will worship God someday.

Why didn't I think the Bible is clear that Jesus will restore all? One reason is I assumed there is a place of never-ending suffering and I read the Bible through that lens. As William James said, *"There's nothing so absurd that if you repeat it often enough, people will believe it."* When I realized this was not taught in the Bible, it became clearer that God will restore all.

Another reason I didn't think the Bible is clear is I looked for clarity in the wrong place—in the verses that describe the judgement of unbelievers (e.g., Rev. 20:15 and the lake of fire). I read the never-ending suffering scenario *into* those verses when, in fact, those verses are inconclusive as to the final fate of those who die as unbelievers.

But then I studied the Scriptures on what happens to people who die as unbelievers. Like many others, I began expecting that Jesus will restore all. When asked, *"Will God save all?"* I started to think: *"I don't know. But I hope so. And there are a lot of good reasons in the Bible to hope so."* Then, as I continued to read the Bible, this hope became a confident expectation.

The Bible is clear that our God is all loving and all powerful. As I looked at the God who sent His Son to die for the sins of the world; as I framed the gospel as Jesus restoring what Adam lost; as I looked at the scores of verses that describe all worshiping God, it became clearer and clearer to me that Jesus will restore all to praise God in the end.

30

Game Changer:

A Different Picture of God

"What comes into our minds when we think about God is the most important thing about us." A.W. Tozer [18]

The message that Jesus restores all was a game changer for me because it affected my view of God. The claim that Jesus will subject 30-60-90% of humans to never-ending suffering is very different from the message that Jesus will restore all to praise God.

We replicate in this life what we think God and heaven are like. A person who believes Jesus will exclude people forever will tend to exclude others now. A person who believes that Jesus restores all is more able to love the unlovable. As a testimony, since Sandy and I began to believe that Jesus will restore all, it has helped us be more patient with each other and more forgiving of others.

---

[18] Tozer, *Knowledge of the Holy*.

This belief affected Abraham Lincoln:

"He did not nor could not believe in the endless punishment of any one of the human race. He understood punishment for sin to be a Bible doctrine; that the punishment was parental in its object, aim, and design, and intended for the good of the offender; hence it must cease when justice is satisfied. He added that all that was lost by the transgression of Adam was made good by the atonement."[19]

Lincoln's belief in Jesus who restores all empowered him to be merciful to others.

The never-ending suffering view has been called the *"alien virus in the body of Christianity, threatening the internal organs."*[20] But the message that Jesus will restore all is a game-changer that transforms the whole world.

---

[19] William J. Wolf, *The Almost Chosen People: A Study of the Religion of Abraham Lincoln* (Garden City, NY: Doubleday, 1959), 104.

[20] Robin A. Parry, "A Response to Michael McClymond's Theological Critique of Universalism," 27.

31

Your Personal Journey

"Behold the Lamb of God who takes away the sin of the world." John 1:29

I did not write this book expecting you to change your opinion based on what I believe. Instead, my hope is that you will take a personal journey in the Scriptures to see if Jesus will restore all.

When I did my study, I thought of my father, Jack Hopler. He grew up in a single parent home and never was reconciled to his dad. My father and I talked often about God. But, to my knowledge, he did not put his faith in Jesus before he died like I had put my faith in Jesus in 1973.

Before I did this study, I thought my father was likely suffering forever, based on the teaching of my church. I assumed I would never see my father again. I also assumed my father and grandfather would never be reunited. However, after my study, I believe Jesus will restore all. I believe my father and grandfather will be reconciled to God and to each other. I believe all three of us will be praising God forever and ever.

I now believe that our risen Savior Jesus Christ, through His judgments, will victoriously restore all humanity to praise God (Rom. 14:9-11):

Jesus: *"Christ died and lived again, that He might be Lord both of the dead and of the living" v. 9.*

Judgment: *"But as for you, why do you judge your brother or sister? Or you as well, why do you regard your brother or sister with contempt? For we will all appear before the judgment seat of God" v.10.*

Victory: *"For it is written: 'As I live, says the Lord, to Me every knee will bow, and every tongue will give praise to God'" v.11.*

But what about you? Do you think your loved ones and all humans who died as unbelievers will be in never-ending torment? Or do you think Jesus will restore them so that, together, you will praise God forever? I ask you to take time to study the Scriptures on this question.

God bless you as you follow the Lord Jesus Christ—the Savior of the world who restores all.

About the Author

John Hopler was born in 1952 in Cleveland, Ohio and grew up in a loving family. He put his faith in Jesus in 1973, while attending The Ohio State University Law School. In 1977, John married the love of his life, Sandy. God has blessed them with 8 children (7 are married) and 13 grandchildren.

John has served as a pastor in four churches and on the boards of three interdenominational ministries: The National Association of Evangelicals, Great Commission Churches and Reliant Mission. He has focused on serving church planters. From the Columbus church he joined in 1975, there are about 50 U.S. churches and 300 international churches (mostly house churches).

Today, John and his wife Sandy share the Jesus-Judgment-Victory gospel and help Christians start churches in their homes.

If you have questions about this booklet or if you want more information about the *Jesus-Judgment Victory* gospel, email John at **jrhopler@gmail.com.**

www.ingramcontent.com/pod-product-compliance
Lightning Source LLC
Chambersburg PA
CBHW071218120626
46546CB00006B/2620